THE
KEY ACCOUNT MANAGER'S
POCKETBOOK

2nd Edition

By Roger E. Jones & Richard J. Ilsley

Drawings by Phil Hailstone

"This compact, easy-to-read book on key account management reduces this complex subject to understandable proportions and easily beats most of the dense, convoluted current texts on the topic."
Professor Malcolm McDonald, Professor of Marketing Planning, Cranfield School of Management

"Building long-term customer-supplier partnerships is the foundation of business success. The Key Account Manager's Pocketbook shows you how to do this using proven strategies and techniques. It is a *must read* business book."
Sahar Hashemi, Co-founder of Coffee Republic and author of *Anyone can do it*

Published by:
Management Pocketbooks Ltd
Laurel House, Station Approach, Alresford, Hants SO24 9JH, U.K.
Tel: +44 (0)1962 735573 Fax: +44 (0)1962 733637
Email: sales@pocketbook.co.uk
Website: www.pocketbook.co.uk

All rights reserved. No part of this publication may be reproduced, stored in a retrieval system or transmitted in any form, or by any means, electronic, mechanical, photocopying, recording or otherwise, without the prior permission of the publishers.

First published 1997 ISBN 9781870471428 © Roger E. Jones

This edition published 2013
ISBN 978 1 906610 59 3
© Roger E. Jones & Richard J. Ilsley

E-book ISBN 978 1 908284 32 7

British Library Cataloguing-in-Publication Data. A catalogue record for this book is available from the British Library.

Design, typesetting and graphics by **efex Ltd**.   Printed in U.K.

CONTENTS

THE KEY ACCOUNT MANAGER 5
Who is a key account manager?, what is a key account?, why a key account is important and different, the role of a key account manager, skills & qualities

THE KEY ACCOUNT AS A BUSINESS PARTNER 15
The benefits, customer perception, the customer perception ladder, climbing the customer perception ladder

DISCOVERING OPPORTUNITIES 27
Opportunities galore, locating them, grouping and prioritising

THE KEY ACCOUNT DEVELOPMENT PLAN 37
What is a key account development plan?, three steps to developing the key account development plan (ADP)

RELATIONSHIP MANAGEMENT 55
Increase your influence, decision making, political environment, organisational map, mirror relationships, leverage opportunities, networking, contact plan

MARKETING COMMUNICATION PROGRAMMES 71
Messages, communication tools, communication plan

WINNING BUSINESS 77
Face-to-face communications, solution selling, proposals, presenting, negotiating

KEY ACCOUNT HANDLING 93
Taking on a new account, getting organised, the key account CRM system, keeping up to date, account meetings and follow-up, handing over an account

The key account manager

THE KEY ACCOUNT MANAGER

WHO IS A KEY ACCOUNT MANAGER?

Anyone who wants to keep and develop business with important customers.

People like: management consultants, accountants, solicitors, merchant bankers, head hunters, surveyors, advertising and PR executives, stockbrokers, retailers and manufacturers of all types, IT and telecom service providers, travel agents, engineers, publishers, trainers, car salesmen, conference organisers, hospitality suppliers, architects, computer programmers, independent tradesmen, haulage contractors, insurance brokers, fund raisers, printers, media specialists, health service providers, etc.

And, most importantly ...
.....**YOU**

THE KEY ACCOUNT MANAGER

WHAT IS A KEY ACCOUNT?

A key account is one of your most important customers - with whom it is crucial to develop and maintain an added value relationship.

To identify which customers are key, decide if the customer/account:

- Is a consistently high revenue producer (remember 20 percent of your customers probably produce 80 percent of your revenue)
- Is offering opportunities to increase sales
- Is looking for a loyal business partner/adviser (you!)
- Is a strategically important industry or market opinion leader

Key accounts keep your business growing

THE KEY ACCOUNT MANAGER

WHY A KEY ACCOUNT IS IMPORTANT

A key account customer offers long-term potential:

- A constant (and growing) stream of high quality revenue
- Reduced sales costs (it is cheaper to grow your business with existing customers than deploy a sales force to find and secure new ones)
- Targeted planning for the future (having a dependable source of sales will enable you to plan investments for your business)
- Improved knowledge of your marketplace (developed via in-depth knowledge of your key account's needs)

Nurture your key accounts

THE KEY ACCOUNT MANAGER

WHY A KEY ACCOUNT IS DIFFERENT

Key account customers differ from your other customers in many ways:

- Your competitors are constantly trying to win them from you
- Multiple decision-makers and many staff influence the buying decision
- An anti-sponsor may exist in the key account - someone who may subtly try to sabotage your sales efforts or relationship
- It is especially important to understand your key account's business
- Strong relationships need to be developed across numerous levels between your two companies

Key accounts are worth the extra effort

THE KEY ACCOUNT MANAGER

THE ROLE OF A KEY ACCOUNT MANAGER
FROM THE KEY ACCOUNT'S PERSPECTIVE

Your key account will expect you to:
- Be the main link into your company for all issues
- Understand its business, market needs and competitive environment
- Help sell them products/services that achieve their business objectives
- Add value to the business relationship with your firm by, for example, acting as a consultant on issues not directly related to your main business
- Help exploit market opportunities and, when possible, identify new and exciting business challenges
- Always act with integrity and in a professional manner

Remember, to your key accounts you are your firm's ambassador

THE KEY ACCOUNT MANAGER

THE ROLE OF A KEY ACCOUNT MANAGER
FROM YOUR FIRM'S PERSPECTIVE

Your firm will expect you to:
- Understand all aspects of the key account's business
- Proactively develop more business with the customer
- Establish strong relationships with the decision makers in your customer's organisation
- Build a wide awareness of your firm's capabilities throughout the key account
- Handle the key account in a professional manner on a day-to-day basis
- Develop a true business partnership with the key account

> Your efforts should make your key account want to rely exclusively on your firm for products/services

THE KEY ACCOUNT MANAGER

SKILLS & QUALITIES

Key Skills
- Planning
- Marketing
- Relationship building
- Problem solving
- Negotiating
- Opportunity creating
- Organisation
- Communication
- Presenting
- Selling

Key Qualities
- Focused
- Diplomatic
- Tenacious
- Flexible
- Independent and team player
- Opportunity seeker

(Juggling is another useful skill since you have to prioritise the needs of the various key accounts you manage)

Adopt a proactive attitude

THE KEY ACCOUNT MANAGER

EXERCISE

- ➤ Consider your own key accounts:
  Why is this customer a key account?
  What are your company's specific expectations and goals for this key account?

- ➤ What are the goals of each key account?
  Define the decision makers and influencers – what does each want?

- ➤ Why should the key account prefer to do business with you rather than your competitors?
  Are you truly differentiated or are you just another competent supplier?

THE KEY ACCOUNT MANAGER

EXERCISE – ADVANCED

➤ Consider your key accounts:
  Summarise your view of the key account's strategy and needs
  Present this to your main key account contact – does he/she agree?

➤ What does 'value' mean for the key account?
  Do you deliver value to the key account?
  How do you know?
  Can you measure the value you are bringing?

➤ Does the key account see you as a strategic partner?
  Do you have a plan to increase your share and margin?

This book will help you to think about all of these critical issues.

THE KEY ACCOUNT AS A BUSINESS PARTNER

THE KEY ACCOUNT AS A BUSINESS PARTNER

ABOUT THIS CHAPTER

Many customers say that they find it hard to differentiate between their top suppliers.

Are you in trouble? Does your customer think you are just another competent supplier? Or worse – are you seen merely as a supplier of a commodity?

To grow your business your key account customer must think of you as a business partner. This chapter will show you how to achieve this; it demonstrates:

- The benefits of forming a key account partnership
- The importance of customer perception
- The significance of the customer perception ladder
- How to climb this ladder to become a true business partner with your key account

THE KEY ACCOUNT AS A BUSINESS PARTNER

THE BENEFITS

If you form a business partnership with your key account you will:

- Profit from a mutually beneficial business dialogue
- Lock out your competitors
- Be able to focus on long-term planning
- Secure a constant and reliable revenue stream

THE KEY ACCOUNT AS A BUSINESS PARTNER

CUSTOMER PERCEPTION

How well you think you are progressing with your account is irrelevant. The key is how well your customer thinks you are doing. Does your customer:

P ick faults with your products?
E njoy discussing business issues with you?
R un when you call?
C onsider you to be the best?
E nter into agreement with your competitors?
P ut off talking to your rivals?
T ick you off from time to time?
I magine you help him succeed?
O pt for competitor products from time to time?
N eed you as much as you need her?

Customer perception is what counts

THE KEY ACCOUNT AS A BUSINESS PARTNER

THE CUSTOMER PERCEPTION LADDER

What level are you at?

Does your customer think you are a:

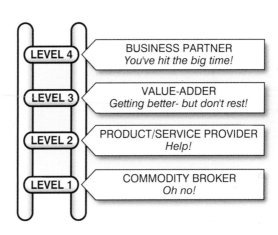

LEVEL 4 — BUSINESS PARTNER
You've hit the big time!

LEVEL 3 — VALUE-ADDER
Getting better- but don't rest!

LEVEL 2 — PRODUCT/SERVICE PROVIDER
Help!

LEVEL 1 — COMMODITY BROKER
Oh no!

THE KEY ACCOUNT AS A BUSINESS PARTNER

THE CUSTOMER PERCEPTION LADDER
LEVEL 1: THE COMMODITY BROKER

To the customer, you are just a commodity supplier. Price is the only factor that influences the purchasing decision. A purchaser of corrugated boxes, for example, might think all manufacturers offer the same product/service and so select based on price alone.

At level 1 you are in trouble because:
- Price sensitivity is sky high
- Customer loyalty is zero

THE KEY ACCOUNT AS A BUSINESS PARTNER

THE CUSTOMER PERCEPTION LADDER
LEVEL 2: THE PRODUCT/SERVICE PROVIDER

To customers you offer a product/service plus some benefits. Price is still the driving factor, though, in distinguishing among competitors' offers. If they think this, then when your competitors allow the customer to print on the corrugated box at no additional charge, your customer will expect you to do the same…and quickly.

Level 2 is only the first step up:
- Price sensitivity is high
- Customer loyalty is low

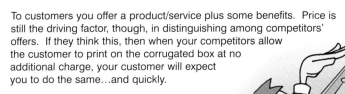

THE KEY ACCOUNT AS A BUSINESS PARTNER

THE CUSTOMER PERCEPTION LADDER
LEVEL 3: THE VALUE-ADDER

In the customers' eyes you add value by helping them achieve their objectives. Take, for example, the banker who helps to finance a customer's new overseas project and also gives advice on exciting opportunities that fit in with the customer's expansion strategy. Slowly but surely you are tying the customer in.

Level 3 is a good position to be in but not the place to stop or, worse, slip! At this level:

- Price sensitivity decreases
- Customer loyalty increases

THE KEY ACCOUNT AS A BUSINESS PARTNER

THE CUSTOMER PERCEPTION LADDER

LEVEL 4: THE BUSINESS PARTNER

You've reached the top! The customer perceives you to be an insider. The strategic advice and insight you provide - as well as your product/service, of course - continually contribute to your customer's success.

At level 4 you have built a solid, long-term relationship:

- Price sensitivity is low
- Customer loyalty is high

THE KEY ACCOUNT AS A BUSINESS PARTNER

CLIMBING THE CUSTOMER PERCEPTION LADDER

Up to Level 2

If your customer perceives that you are at level 1, a commodity broker, you can climb to level 2 to become a product/service provider by:

- **Differentiating your service from your competition.** For example, a manufacturer of paper cups was able to add a short run flexible printing service at little additional cost to give the customer the ability to use the cup as a promotional tool
- **Selling the benefits of your product/service.** For example, a consumer goods manufacturer gained extra distribution and sales in smaller grocery shops by demonstrating to store owners that its consumer TV campaign would bring in more customers, if they placed advertising material and focused displays in the store

Up to Level 3

You can jump from level 2 to level 3, a value-adder, by:

- **Simply setting account objectives that mirror your customer's business objectives.** This will ensure that your efforts focus on creating real value for your key account.

THE KEY ACCOUNT AS A BUSINESS PARTNER

CLIMBING THE CUSTOMER PERCEPTION LADDER

Up to Level 4

To reach level 4, a strategic business partnership, you must follow the steps described in this book:

- Discover opportunities within your key account
- Set account objectives and strategies that will help both you and your key account grow
- Design key account plans that will help you structure your planning
- Develop strong relationships with decision makers and political high flyers, to position yourself strategically within the key account organisation
- Generate strong positive awareness of your firm throughout the key account
- Win new business with your key account
- Proactively and professionally handle the key account on a day-to-day basis

THE KEY ACCOUNT AS A BUSINESS PARTNER

EXERCISE

- ➤ Ask yourself where you think you stand on the customer perception ladder.

- ➤ More importantly, where does your key account think you and each of your competitors stand on the perception ladder?

- ➤ List the reasons for your current position on the perception ladder.

- ➤ If you are not yet at level 4 then, before reading further, write down the practical steps you think you can take to climb the ladder. These might include: starting to actively differentiate your product/service, developing a closer understanding of your key account's decision-making process, and improving your image in the eyes of the customer by handling the business more proactively.

Discovering Opportunities

DISCOVERING OPPORTUNITIES

OPPORTUNITIES GALORE

Your key account is full of opportunities. For example, opportunities to:

- Develop more business
- Learn about the marketplace
- Discover new information
- Meet influential people

Let's discover how to locate opportunities and then focus on opportunities that can be found from looking at your key accounts' business objectives, their (and your) competitors and sales figures.

DISCOVERING OPPORTUNITIES

LOCATING THEM (1)

The simplest way to find opportunities is to ...

ASK YOUR KEY ACCOUNT ...

... how they think you can win new business with them, improve service levels, get closer to their subsidiaries, etc.

DISCOVERING OPPORTUNITIES

LOCATING THEM (2)

Be a detective and look for opportunities:

- At trade fairs
- In the trade press
- By talking to your key account's customers and other suppliers
- In market research reports

DISCOVERING OPPORTUNITIES

LOCATING THEM (3)

When thinking about your key accounts and their/your competitors, you can find more opportunities by 'SWOT'-ting each.

List their:

      Strengths

        Weaknesses

          Opportunities

            Threats

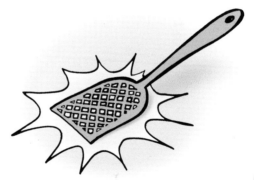

DISCOVERING OPPORTUNITIES

VIA YOUR KEY ACCOUNT'S OBJECTIVES

Ask your key account customers:

- "What are your organisation's objectives for the next year/five years?" (don't rely on customers' annual reports for this information - they mostly say the same)
- "What do you need to help achieve those objectives?"

EXERCISE

➤ List what you can do to help them achieve their objectives.

DISCOVERING OPPORTUNITIES

VIA YOUR KEY ACCOUNT'S COMPETITORS

Ask your key account customers:

- "How do you view your competitors?"
- "How are you going to stay ahead of the pack?"
- "What can I do to help you?"

EXERCISE

➤ List how you can help your key account keep its edge.

DISCOVERING OPPORTUNITIES

VIA YOUR COMPETITORS

Ask your key account customers:

- "What do you think of my competitors?"
- "What do you think of our strengths, weaknesses, opportunities and threats, compared with those of our competitors?"

EXERCISE

- ➤ List the strengths, weaknesses, opportunities and threats of each of your competitors.
- ➤ List the opportunities you have with which to differentiate yourself from your competitors.

DISCOVERING OPPORTUNITIES

VIA SALES INFORMATION

The basics of life are too often ignored. Think about:

- **Sales figures** - Are they going up (or down) and why? Are you responding appropriately? Is your competition hot on your tail?
- **Past successes** - Why did you succeed? Was your service quality best? Were your financial terms unbeatable? Luck?
- **Past failures** - Don't be bashful - admit to past failures! Was your proposal lousy? Was your relationship with the decision makers not up to scratch?
  Tip If your sales pitch fails, always ask your key account the reasons why. Learn from your failures.

EXERCISE

➤ List the reasons for your successes and failures over the past year.

➤ What can you learn from your past sales successes and failures?

➤ Ask your key account customer how you can increase sales.

DISCOVERING OPPORTUNITIES

GROUPING & PRIORITISING

- **Group** your opportunities into those that will help you:
    - increase usage or sell more of your existing product/service
    - win new business, eg: sales to new parts of your customer's organisation
    - improve your service levels
    - build strong relationships

- **Prioritise** the opportunities by thinking about what you will need in terms of:
    - time, staff and money to achieve each
    - what the return/profit will be from each

THE KEY ACCOUNT DEVELOPMENT PLAN

THE KEY ACCOUNT DEVELOPMENT PLAN

WHAT IS THIS PLAN?

It is:

- A tool with which to achieve effective, efficient, added-value key account management
- An often forgotten step for planning strategy with your key account
- The place where you record all important objectives and actions regarding the development of your business with the account
- The ready reference for all colleagues involved
- The place where you get the long-term view on how your business is going to evolve and how to reach targets

THE KEY ACCOUNT DEVELOPMENT PLAN

3 STEPS TO DEVELOPING THE PLAN

1. **Set key account objectives** - what you want to achieve and by when
2. **Develop key strategies and tactics** - how you are going to achieve each objective
3. **Write the key account development plan** - put it all together in an easy to follow format

THE KEY ACCOUNT DEVELOPMENT PLAN

STEP 1: SET KEY ACCOUNT OBJECTIVES
WHAT IS AN OBJECTIVE?

An objective simply states what you want to achieve and by when.

The objectives you choose should be based on your top seven opportunities.

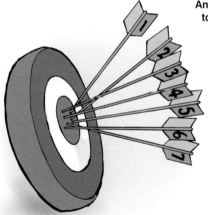

THE KEY ACCOUNT DEVELOPMENT PLAN

STEP 1: SET KEY ACCOUNT OBJECTIVES

When setting objectives:

- Mirror your key account's objectives

    For example, if you are a book publisher and your retail bookshop customer wants to launch a mail order service targeted to pensioners, then your objectives might be threefold:

    a) to help in an added-value fashion by supplying market research on their target market segment

    b) to develop an internal inventory management process to respond quickly to small yet regular orders from your customer

    c) to create a new range of home craft books and get 10 percent of mail order sales within six months of its launch

Set objectives that will help you climb the customer perception ladder

THE KEY ACCOUNT DEVELOPMENT PLAN

STEP 1: SET KEY ACCOUNT OBJECTIVES

When setting objectives:

Make sure the objectives you set for your key account conform to the requirements of your company. So for example, if your company wants more share, then you need objectives to reflect this.

- Design them to:
  a) increase existing sales, share, margin or whatever your company needs
  b) win new business
  c) improve service levels
  d) build strong relationships
- Identify seven annual objectives
- Try to prioritise them according to your key account's main priorities

Always involve your customer when developing the plan

THE KEY ACCOUNT DEVELOPMENT PLAN

STEP 1: SET KEY ACCOUNT OBJECTIVES

EXERCISE

- How do you currently set your key account objectives?
- List your objectives for each of your key accounts.
- Do your objectives mirror those of your customer?
- Sit back and think - are these objectives realistic and achievable?
- Are they prioritised according to your customers' main priorities?

> Make sure your objectives are quantifiable (whenever possible) and state when you are going to achieve them

THE KEY ACCOUNT DEVELOPMENT PLAN

STEP 2: DEVELOP STRATEGIES & TACTICS

Remember:

- Key account development strategies:
    - set out the means to achieve key account objectives
    - consider the resources - human & financial - needed to implement each strategy

- Tactics:
    - are specific actions designed to achieve a strategy
    - must be performed over a defined time period (eg: per quarter)

> Don't forget, your colleagues' input will add value to your strategy

THE KEY ACCOUNT DEVELOPMENT PLAN

STEP 2: DEVELOP STRATEGIES & TACTICS

When devising strategies for each of your objectives, think whether you need to:

- Revamp the product/service you provide
- Alter the price at which it is sold
- Promote your offer to the key account in a different way
- Change the place you sell it
- Obtain extra resources

> When developing key account strategies, ask yourself:
> how am I going to block my competitors' efforts?

THE KEY ACCOUNT DEVELOPMENT PLAN

STEP 2: DEVELOP STRATEGIES & TACTICS
PRODUCT/SERVICE

Do you need to:

- Change the design?
- Stress other benefits?
- Develop a completely new offering?
- Phase out a product/service?
- Sell different quantities?

EXERCISE

➤ List how you need to adjust your product/service in order to achieve each of your key account objectives.

THE KEY ACCOUNT DEVELOPMENT PLAN

STEP 2: DEVELOP STRATEGIES & TACTICS

PRICE

Do you need to:

- Price low to get a greater share of your key account's business and deter your competitors from copying your product/service offering? (Warning - once you offer a low price it's very difficult to increase it later.)
- Offer a new product/service at a high initial price in order to maximise your profits? (Warning - your competitors will quickly copy your new product/service and probably offer it at a lower price.)
- Trim your product/service to maintain your margins?
- Bundle your offer or separate it into individual elements?

EXERCISE

➤ Consider whether your current pricing policy needs to change to help you achieve your key account objectives.

THE KEY ACCOUNT DEVELOPMENT PLAN

STEP 2: DEVELOP STRATEGIES & TACTICS

PROMOTION

Promotion is about how you are going to use communication effectively to achieve your key account objectives.

For a key account manager, the best communication opportunities can be:

- Meetings
- Presentations/seminars
- Trade shows
- Public relations
- Sponsorship
- Internal newsletters

EXERCISE

➤ Itemise the promotion methods you currently use and indicate how effective they are.

➤ Can you think of any other communication opportunities?

Note Communicating effectively with your key account is essential - see later chapters.

THE KEY ACCOUNT DEVELOPMENT PLAN

STEP 2: DEVELOP STRATEGIES & TACTICS

PLACE

Place is the location where you supply your product/service to your customer.
To achieve your key account objectives you may need to:

- Change your distribution methods
- Enhance your quality control procedures
- Review practices with your distributor
- Reduce costs by outsourcing deliveries
- Seek additional channels
- Make better use of new technology

EXERCISE

➤ Consider whether your distribution strategy affects your ability to achieve your key account objectives.

➤ When was the last time you reviewed your distribution methods?

THE KEY ACCOUNT DEVELOPMENT PLAN

STEP 2: DEVELOP STRATEGIES & TACTICS

RESOURCES

Ensure your strategies are achievable by evaluating your:

- **People**
  - Do you have enough staff available?
  - Do they have the right skill sets or need re-training?

- **Time**
  - Is your time planning realistic?
  - Are there any calendar constraints?

- **Money**
  - Is the budget available to implement your strategies and tactics?

EXERCISE

➤ For each of your strategies, list the current (or extra) resources you are going to need and when you are going to use them.

THE KEY ACCOUNT DEVELOPMENT PLAN

STEP 2: DEVELOP STRATEGIES & TACTICS

TACTICS

Break down your strategy into specific actions that must be performed over a defined time period (eg: per quarter).

Here, for example, is the case of a graphic design firm looking to improve service levels to a key corporate account:

Objective: Reduce the turnaround time for the production of corporate brochures from 60 days to 30 days.

Strategy: Act as a technology consultant to account's in-house publications department.

Tactics: Quarter 1: Evaluate in-house processes and propose improvements.

Quarter 2: Upgrade in-house technology as necessary and provide training.

Quarter 3: Monitor the department's progress.

Quarter 4: Together, evaluate new production trends and develop plans for the coming year.

THE KEY ACCOUNT DEVELOPMENT PLAN

STEP 3: WRITING THE PLAN

Account development plans (ADPs) detail your objectives, strategies and tactics in an easy-to-follow format, helping you to manage your efforts on behalf of your key account.

Remember:

Achieve measurable increase in business
Develop long-term business relationships
Profit from opportunities
Strengthen communication with customer

Focus efforts to help you (and your customer) grow
Organise internal resources
Create awareness of your product/service within the account
Understand customer's business environment
Solicit interest in your customer among your senior management

ADPs focus your business development efforts

THE KEY ACCOUNT DEVELOPMENT PLAN

STEP 3: WRITING THE PLAN

EXERCISE

Using a template like the one on the next page:

➤ Write your account objectives down the left hand column. For example, if you are a key account manager for a telecommunications company and your account is a growing international bank, an objective might be to: 'Deploy system XK in foreign exchange division by 3rd quarter.'

➤ State three strategies you are going to initiate to achieve your objective.
For example: a) carry out full user needs analysis, b) reduce service call-out times from 3 hours to 1.5 hours, and c) agree revised pricing model with customer.

➤ Then for each quarter, alongside each strategy, write down your tactics.
For example, for action a) the tactics might be: Quarter 1 - perform user workshop; Quarter 2 - evaluate results with customer; Quarter 3 - carry out any necessary product enhancements; Quarter 4 - test enhanced system.

➤ At the bottom of the template note other key dates - customer's conferences, in-house seminars, sector events, etc.

THE KEY ACCOUNT DEVELOPMENT PLAN

STEP 3: WRITING THE PLAN

EXERCISE TEMPLATE

Last updated on xx/yy/zz   Account Name: _____

OBJECTIVES	STRATEGIES	TACTICS			
		Q1	Q2	Q3	Q4
1.	A)				
	B)				
	C)				
2.	A)				
	B)				
	C)				
3.	A)				
	B)				
	C)				
4.	A)				
	B)				
	C)				
5.	A)				
	B)				
	C)				
6.	A)				
	B)				
	C)				
7.	A)				
	B)				
	C)				
Other Key Dates					

Relationship Management

RELATIONSHIP MANAGEMENT
INCREASE YOUR INFLUENCE

The key to successful relationship management is to increase your influence with the decision maker in your key account. To do this you must:

- Know the messages you want to communicate
- Find out who's who in the decision making process
- Understand the 'internal politics' in your customer's organisation
- Find your way around the key account company by drawing an 'organisational map'
- Initiate 'mirror relationships'
- Utilise 'leverage opportunities' whenever possible
- 'Network' in the key account and so become familiar with the whole organisation
- Develop and implement a 'contact plan'

RELATIONSHIP MANAGEMENT
KNOWING WHAT TO COMMUNICATE

Before you start your relationship management programme, you must first establish the messages you want your key account to take on board and the reasons why. The message needs to be:

How your product/service offer helps your key account to succeed

EXERCISE

- List components of your product/service offer.
- By each, state how their benefits help your key account to be more successful, for example: 'Our new accounting software package speeds transactions by 30 per cent which means that your accounting staff are now 30 per cent more efficient'.

Think about what the customer needs but also how your offer is differentiated versus your competitors' offers – there is little benefit in an offer which meets the customer's needs but is the same as the competition.

RELATIONSHIP MANAGEMENT

DECISION MAKING

PEOPLE TYPES (1)

Find out who within your key account is the:

- **Decision maker**
    - signs-off on all strategy and deals. It varies depending on who you talk to, so ask a few different people within the account "Who makes the final decision?" and then decide yourself

    Develop a rapport with this person if you can

- **Influencer**
    - influences the decision maker
    - has expertise in a particular area - finance, strategy, operations, information technology, etc.
    - gives valued input to the decision maker

    Make sure this person is on your side

RELATIONSHIP MANAGEMENT

DECISION MAKING
PEOPLE TYPES (2)

Find out who within your key account is the:

- **Sponsor**
    - feeds you with non-confidential information on what is happening within the key account
    - tells you who's who and who does what within the account
    - may suggest business development ideas to you

    Solicit this person's help judiciously and offer added value information in return

- **Anti-sponsor**
    - watch out! ... there is one in every company
    - promotes your competitors' products/services only
    - is typically negative to all your ideas and even tries to block your efforts

    Try to develop at least a neutral relationship with this person

Important note These people groupings often overlap. For example, the decision maker for a smaller purchase may only be an influencer for the bigger purchase; a sponsor may also be an influencer.

RELATIONSHIP MANAGEMENT

CUSTOMER POLITICS (1)

Understanding the political environment within your key account will give you valuable insight into such things as:

- Why decisions do (or don't) go your way
- Whether your main contact is on his way up (or out of) the organisation
- Who holds the real power

To do this you must think of the people within your customer's organisation in terms of 'political groupings', namely:

The Top Gun

- A top decision maker - managing director, functional director, or maybe the department head
- The power in the organisation is centred here - with one person or several
- Has the organisational trappings that go with being a big shooter; for example: big office, big budget, lots of staff and lots of responsibility
- Never upset a top gun; long-lasting memories make for slow forgiveness

RELATIONSHIP MANAGEMENT

CUSTOMER POLITICS (2)
POLITICAL GROUPINGS

The Rising Star

- Is rapidly climbing the organisational ladder
- The star rises normally via a mentor - someone that coaches and guides (often a top gun)
- Become associated with a rising star - her progress upwards will help yours
- Rising stars are trusted by the top guns so they can help get key information to you quickly

The Fallen Star

- Maybe a protected species, kept on for 'old times sake' or originally recruited by a top gun (who has been secretly regretting it ever since)
- Maybe suffering from the Peter Principle that states - 'people get promoted to their level of incompetence'
- Has limited influence within the organisation
- Is normally by-passed when decisions are made

RELATIONSHIP MANAGEMENT

CUSTOMER POLITICS (3)
POLITICAL GROUPINGS

The Fox

- Can be sly, move quickly, and attack at the right time
- Is hard to spot, working quietly behind the scenes and not engaged in open battles
- Normally has a good network of connections within the company, especially with a top gun

The Foot Soldier

- One of the mass of people within the key account
- Maybe an aspiring top gun
- Enlist support here (all top guns and rising stars were once foot soldiers)

EXERCISE

➤ List the people in your key account according to these 'political groupings'.

➤ Which group does your main contact fall into?

➤ Do you know a rising star? If not, consider how you can become more closely associated with one.

RELATIONSHIP MANAGEMENT

ORGANISATIONAL MAP (1)

A map helps you navigate and plan travel. An 'organisational map' will help you to find your way around your key account. It will enable you to identify:

- The people groupings - decision making and political - in your key account

- Those with whom you should develop 'mirror relationships'

- Networking opportunities

RELATIONSHIP MANAGEMENT

ORGANISATIONAL MAP (2)

Follow these simple rules to map out your key account's organisation:

1. Draw an organisational chart of the company, indicating names and job titles. For example:

Key Account 'A' - organisational map

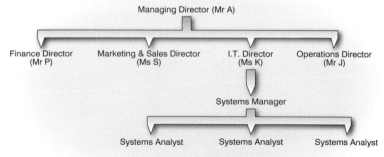

RELATIONSHIP MANAGEMENT

ORGANISATIONAL MAP (3)

More rules to map out your key account's organisation:

2. Mark in red your main contact
3. In a different colour show who is a decision maker (DM) influencer (I), sponsor (S) or anti-sponsor (AS) for your product/service
4. Now note the political roles each has: TG = top gun; RS = rising star (and M = his/her mentor); FLS = fallen star; F = fox; and FTS = foot soldier
5. Show the main linkages - who is aligned with whom

RELATIONSHIP MANAGEMENT

ORGANISATIONAL MAP (4)

Key Account 'A' - organisational map

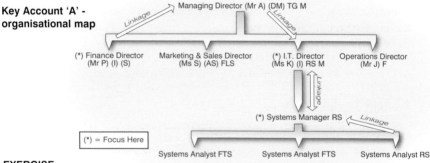

(*) = Focus Here

EXERCISE

- See if you can identify any people groupings.
- Are any foot soldiers closely linked with rising stars?
- Where does your main contact fit into this map?

RELATIONSHIP MANAGEMENT

MIRROR RELATIONSHIPS

To build a stronger bond with your key account, ensure 'mirror relationships' are developed.

Mirror relationships result when staff at the same functional level within both organisations - yours and your key account's - have built up a rapport. Such relationships can exist between, for example:

- managing director and managing director
- technical director and technical director
- finance director and finance director
- product specialist and product specialist

Key benefit: If the managing directors build a good rapport, then you are likely to obtain political acceptance for your business proposition. As a result, senior management on both sides are more likely to buy into your ideas.

How can they meet? The opportunities are numerous: eg: trade events, conferences, a meeting, company golfing day, etc.

Tip Give your colleagues briefing notes and a list of key messages they need to convey before they meet their counterparts.

RELATIONSHIP MANAGEMENT

LEVERAGE OPPORTUNITIES

'Leverage opportunities' occur when an outside body can lobby or influence your key account on your behalf. Outside bodies could include:

- Your key account's shareholders
- Non-competing suppliers
- Your shareholders
- Trade organisations
- Consultants

Messages to get across might include: you can't be more generous than your current financial offer; your expansion plans are backed by a firm financial base; and there is glowing industry feedback on your new product/service.

EXERCISE

➤ Identify how you can use 'leverage opportunities'.

➤ Are there any business links between your shareholders and your key accounts?

➤ Do you have a rapport with any of your key account's non-competing suppliers?

RELATIONSHIP MANAGEMENT

NETWORKING

Successful key account managers have a wide base of influential contacts within their key account, in addition to their main day-to-day contact. To get to know more people, 'network', ie: get someone to introduce you to a person who introduces you to someone else, etc. Here's how to network:

- List the people you want to meet in your key account; e.g. a rising star that may have influence over your product/service area in the future or a decision maker for one of the subsidiaries
- List options to meet them, such as:
  - via your sponsor or main day-to-day contact
  - by invitation to your marketing communication events - seminar, exhibition, etc
  - by asking one of your key account's other suppliers to introduce you
- Aim to meet as many people as appropriate, but do not go behind the back of your main day-to-day contact

RELATIONSHIP MANAGEMENT

CONTACT PLAN

Relationship management will, like all business activities, benefit from being handled in a systematic planned manner. So:

- Know who are the decision makers
- Learn the internal politics
- Define your key messages
- Develop an organisational map and initiate 'mirror relationships'
- Identify and action your 'networking' and 'leverage' opportunities

Marketing communication programmes

MARKETING COMMUNICATION PROGRAMMES

PROGRAMME'S FUNCTION

Key Account Managers need to develop, whenever possible, a marketing communication programme to:

- Build widespread awareness of their product/service throughout the key account
- Convey information about the evolution of their offer
- Strengthen their strategic business relationship

To do this you must:

- Define the messages you wish to communicate
- Select the best communication tools

MARKETING COMMUNICATION PROGRAMMES

THE MESSAGES

Typical messages deal with:

- Your company - size, market share, innovations and expertise
- Your product/service offer - benefits, current range and planned developments
- Trends in your key account's business sector
- Critical market issues facing your key account (and how you can help) such as:
  - technological changes
  - customer demographics
  - government regulations
  - new competitors
  - environmental issues

MARKETING COMMUNICATION PROGRAMMES

COMMUNICATION TOOLS (1)

Options include:

Newsletter

- Many companies have an internal newsletter or magazine
- See if you (or your PR department) can include a regular article or column
- Rather than an advertisement, make the column an added value feature that leaves readers thinking they learned something from it

Customer email bulletin

- Create your own email for your key account
- Keep it brief and informative

Seminar

- Organise a seminar for your key account on a relevant topic
- Gain the support of your main contact, agree on the attendee list, choose whether to do the administration yourself or use a consultant and ask for feedback to determine its effectiveness

MARKETING COMMUNICATION PROGRAMMES

COMMUNICATION TOOLS (2)

Options include:

Company conference
- Ask if you can speak (or run a workshop) at the account's annual conference
- Try to arrange a good slot - first thing in the morning - to avoid the graveyard session just after lunch
- Look for sponsorship opportunities - the printed programme, a dinner, etc

Trade conference
- Speak at or run a workshop at an industry trade conference to help demonstrate that your company is an opinion leader

Write a blog and/or industry media articles
- High value blogs will be sent on to others and having articles published on the right website or publication will enhance your credibility as an expert. You can use the copy in your key account email

Corporate hospitality
- From motor racing to croquet
- A great way to network

MARKETING COMMUNICATION PROGRAMMES

EXAMPLE PROGRAMME

Consider what marketing communication methods you use. If they are carried out in a haphazard fashion rather than planned, then develop a communication programme. Here is an example:

Objective: to ensure all staff within the key account understand our strength in new technologies. To get this message across, the following programme is suggested:

Quarter 1	• Email article on expertise of our research team • Press article on launch of product XYZ
Quarter 2	• Speak at customer's regional conference on how new technologies can improve internal efficiencies
Quarter 3	• Hold seminar on emerging technologies and how to manage them
Quarter 4	• Speak at key account's annual convention on prioritising technology investment decisions • Host a corporate hospitality event at Science Museum where guests can participate in technology-based games evening

Winning business

WINNING BUSINESS

SEIZING OPPORTUNITIES

Discovering opportunities and developing your key account development plan are central to developing business with your key account.
But, how do you seize the new business opportunities?

The only way is to:

- Perfect your face-to-face communication skills
- Sell solutions
- Write convincing proposals
- Give winning presentations
- Negotiate effectively

WINNING BUSINESS

FACE-TO-FACE COMMUNICATIONS
ACTIVE LISTENING

The most successful sales people spend as much time listening as they do talking. Try the following to improve your listening skills:

- **Don't interrupt;** let the other person finish speaking before talking
- **Relax;** if you feel tense and uptight you are unlikely to listen effectively
- Try to **understand the other person's point of view**, even if you don't agree with it
- Show you are listening by **paraphrasing** what the speaker has said
- **Take notes sparingly**, it's difficult to write and listen at the same time
- Try to **avoid distractions**

> Active listening helps you show empathy

WINNING BUSINESS

FACE-TO-FACE COMMUNICATIONS
RAPPORT BUILDING

Words

- Use words similar to those being spoken by the other person:
    - if enthusiastic and expansive, then use words loaded with emotion like 'great', 'vital'
    - if concise and precise, then use planning words like 'decide', 'agree', 'progress'

Pace

- Match the pace of other person's speech

Body language

- Mirror (but don't mimic) your customer's body posture

> The key is to 'match' the other person's personality

WINNING BUSINESS

SOLUTION SELLING (1)

Solving problems

- **P**robe problems - are they key?
- **A**mount - how much is it costing them?
- **P**rioritise - how big an issue is it for them?
- **A**ctions - what have they done about it?
- **S**olution - can you present one?
- **A**sk - how to move forward?

> Key account managers sell solutions to the customer's problems

WINNING BUSINESS

SOLUTION SELLING (2)

Probe problems
- Ask questions that explore the difficulties and dissatisfactions your key account is experiencing, in areas where your product/service can help
  For example: "Are you worried about your assembly line down-time?"

Amount
- Ask questions to find out the amount each problem is costing your key account in money terms
  For example, if the assembly line breaks down for two hours every week, ask questions that identify the true cost of this problem to the business (including any clients lost because of it): "Having your assembly line down for two hours every week must mean that your operators are also idle for this time and, importantly, you lose two hours' production each week?" Then get your customer to quantify this in money terms:

	(2 hours x number of staff x salaries)
+	(2 hours lost production)
+	(extra overtime to get through backlogs)
=	total cost per week

WINNING BUSINESS

SOLUTION SELLING (3)

Prioritise

- With your customer, prioritise the business problems you discuss according to how much money each problem is costing

Actions

- Establish what has been done about each problem. Were the various actions successful?

> Problem solvers win more business

WINNING BUSINESS

SOLUTION SELLING (4)

Solution

- If you can, present a solution to the problem
  For example, if your assembly line has a 99.99 per cent up-time performance, ask:
  "Would you be interested in a solution that might save you over $10,000 a week?"
  The only thing they are going to say is "YES!"

Ask

- Ask - many people forget to; ask if you can implement your solution and agree a timetable

> People like talking about problems if you offer them solutions

WINNING BUSINESS

PROPOSALS
STRUCTURE & CONTENT

Proposals must be easy to follow and logical. Try this general format:

Executive summary	-	one page summary of the proposal
Introduction	-	state how you were asked to submit the bid
Statement of experience	-	record your business dealings, including those with other non-competing customers of a similar size
Product/service offering	-	stress how your product/service benefits will help
Customer support	-	detail the back-up facilities you can provide
Costings	-	leave yourself room to negotiate
Timing	-	indicate how long your proposal is valid for
Appendices	-	include technical details, project plans, referrals

> A logical structure makes for easier reading

WINNING BUSINESS

PROPOSALS
STYLE & LENGTH

Easy to read proposals are always well received, so:

Plan	- make an outline before you start writing
Be brief and punchy	- if unsure whether to include a fact or piece of information, then leave it out
	- aim for 10 pages maximum, if possible
Minimise fog factor	- use short words, short sentences and bullet points

Keep proposals simple

WINNING BUSINESS

PRESENTING

14 KEYS TO SUCCESS

1. **Know your audience**
   - what do they want to hear?
2. **Adopt one theme with three messages**
   - build up an argument that leads to an irresistible conclusion
3. **Summarise, summarise, summarise**
   - to reinforce your three messages
4. **Don't be a bore**
   - never talk for more than 8 minutes on a topic; summarise, then move on
5. **Signpost**
   - show an agenda slide after each topic so your audience can see how far they have travelled through your presentation and what lies ahead
6. **Present word pictures and strong visual aids**
   - reinforce your message and help conjure up mental images
7. **Use cards**
   - to remember the sequence and key points (never a script)

WINNING BUSINESS

PRESENTING

14 KEYS TO SUCCESS (cont'd)

8. **Encourage participation**
   - to motivate your audience (try a quiz, allow questions or ask their opinions)
9. **Start powerfully**
   - begin strongly and confidently to grab your audience's attention and interest
10. **Rehearse**
    - in front of friends and colleagues; ask for feedback
11. **Make eye contact**
    - glance around the room in a 'W' motion
12. **Check posture**
    - be natural, but stand up straight to feel more confident
13. **Check the room**
    - know the layout and facilities, including how the audio visual equipment works
14. **Go for it!**
    - the more you rehearse, the more confident you will be; and the more presentations you give, the better you will become

WINNING BUSINESS

NEGOTIATING

When do you negotiate? After your key account has decided to buy from you. The next task will be to negotiate the terms and conditions, and possibly elements of your product/service offering. This is a six step process:

Step 1 - Prepare

- List overall benefits of the deal to you - qualitative and quantitative
- Identify individual components of the deal, and the cost of each to you
- Itemise the small things you may trade and prioritise them
- Itemise the big things you won't trade
- Fix the bottom line - the point at which you will say "no" and walk away
- List the above from your key account's perspective too

> Better deals are made by better prepared negotiators

WINNING BUSINESS

NEGOTIATING

Step 2 - Establish the playing field
- Ask up front what deal is ideal
- State what you can give
- Identify areas of common ground

Step 3 - Probe
- Find out how important the things wanted are and prioritise them
- Ask 'what if' questions

Step 4 - Propose
- Propose a solution that meets your mutual aims and expectations
- State when you have no freedom to move
- Stress long-term benefits
- Emphasise value, not $$$

Know when to say "NO"

WINNING BUSINESS

NEGOTIATING

Step 5 - Trade
- Make small concessions seem BIG
- Know when to stop
- Never give away points, always trade

Step 6 - Agree
- Confirm what has been agreed
- Ensure both parties agree
- Put it in writing

Tips
- always aim high
- take time to think
- be confident
- if you reach a deadlock, take a break

If they say "YES" straight away, you have probably given too much away

WINNING BUSINESS

NEGOTIATING

Recognise your customer's style:

Salami slice	-	when you thought you had agreed, he comes back and asks for more
Best offer	-	asks for your best deal immediately; don't give it as she will want to come back and negotiate anyway
Mr Tough Guy	-	slams hand on the table and shouts, "It's not good enough"; don't be scared, just respond in a professional manner
Yorkshire terrier	-	just like the dog, the customer keeps barking for more; only trade small concessions, and then only when you really have to
Oh no!	-	simply doesn't like negotiating; don't be too hard on these customers

What's your key account's style?

KEY ACCOUNT HANDLING

KEY ACCOUNT HANDLING

AREAS OF FOCUS

Key account handling is about the day-to-day management of your key customer account. To do this in a professional and proactive manner you must focus on the following areas:

- Taking on a new key account
- The key account profile
- Getting organised
- The key account CRM system
- Keeping up to date
- Reviewing the Account Development Plan (ADP)
- Internal communication
- Account meetings
- Account follow-up
- Handing over an account (or what to do when the project ends)

Business partners get involved

KEY ACCOUNT HANDLING

TAKING ON A NEW KEY ACCOUNT (1)

This can happen either because 1) the existing account manager moves on; or 2) you win a new key account customer.

1. The existing account manager moves on and you inherit the customer.
   The secret of being accepted as the new key account manager is to:

- Ensure your boss has explained the reasons for the change to your key account's senior management
- Make certain the outgoing key account manager briefs you fully on all issues and then STAYS OUT!
- Review the ADP
- Meet your key account contact and discuss current activities
- Tell everyone relevant in your company of the change
- Get involved in a new project if you can

> Be proactive from day one

KEY ACCOUNT HANDLING

TAKING ON A NEW KEY ACCOUNT (2)

2. You win a new key account customer. Congratulations, now:
- Hold a kick-off meeting to start the planning
- Ensure mutual expectations are expressed and matched
- Try and have an early achievable success
- Develop an ADP
- Start relationship management activities from week one
- Brief your colleagues on your new key account's importance
- Establish clear lines of communication
- Be the main point of entry into your company

> Speak often to your key account contact and develop a personal rapport

KEY ACCOUNT HANDLING

THE KEY ACCOUNT PROFILE

Make a key information profile of your key account; include:

- Name and full company contact details
- Head office decision maker, influencer(s), sponsor and anti-sponsor contact details
- Current sales volumes - keep this figure up to date
- Planned growth of your business in next budget cycle
- Three main strengths the key account has over its competitors
- Three main weaknesses the key account has over its competitors
- Names of your top competitors and their main opportunities with your key account

> If your key account's performance is falling behind that of your other customers, find out why ... you may both be missing a business opportunity

KEY ACCOUNT HANDLING

GETTING ORGANISED (1)

You will only become a winning key account manager if you first get organised. Try these tips:

- **Clarify objectives** — do this with your boss so you don't waste time on minor tasks
- **Prioritise your work** — into **A** - must do; **B** - should do; and **C** - could do
- **Write daily 'to do' lists** — calls to make, e-mails to send and tasks to begin/complete
- **Plan projects** — in advance and review regularly
- **Break projects down into a series of smaller tasks** — remember Parkinson's Law states that the 'work expands to fill the time available', so set deadlines for each task

GET ORGANISED - and you will be more effective

KEY ACCOUNT HANDLING

GETTING ORGANISED (2)

- **Be ruthless with your filing** - throw away everything you are not going to need again
- **Follow-through is the key** - if you have been out visiting your key accounts, allocate sufficient time to action the follow-up work
- **Make phone calls first thing in the morning** - arrange call back times if necessary
- **Organise your desk** - messy desk = messy work

**GET ORGANISED -
spring-clean your desk and files today**

KEY ACCOUNT HANDLING

GETTING ORGANISED (3)

- **Prioritise your reading** — If it doesn't look interesting or relevant delete it
- **Keep a separate file for each key account**
- **Have a file containing all outstanding items** — with target completion dates on each
- **Update your CRM system every time you interact with the key account**
- **Review sales figures** — do this as frequently as relevant; daily, weekly or monthly
- **Don't leave tasks incomplete** — they will always catch up on you

GET ORGANISED - start today, your colleagues and customers will soon notice the difference

KEY ACCOUNT HANDLING

THE KEY ACCOUNT CRM SYSTEM (1)

A tool for effective personal planning. When using your CRM system, include...

F ollow-up actions - put in bold
O bjectives with target completion dates
L ist times and dates for next customer calls
L ook for opportunities at conferences, etc.
O rganise tasks according to customer priorities
W arning signs - put in red - when projects slip

> FOLLOW through is the key

KEY ACCOUNT HANDLING

THE KEY ACCOUNT CRM SYSTEM (2)

Your Customer Relationship Management (CRM) system is a powerful tool for managing your key account.

- Use your CRM system to maintain an up-to-date profile, to plan your activities and to generate progress reports

- Using the right software tool also allows you to share your key account knowledge and plans with your line manager and colleagues – similarly you can view their information

This helps sharing of key account knowledge and best practice throughout the company.

KEY ACCOUNT HANDLING

KEEPING UP TO DATE

Why?	• Be an expert • Add value	• Keep one step ahead
About what?	• Your key account's activities • Their competitors • Their other suppliers	• Their end customers • Your competitors • The economy
How?	• Trade press • Trade shows and conferences • Market research reports • National press	• Your colleagues • Public libraries • Industry associations • Industry blogs

Always know the key issues of the day

KEY ACCOUNT HANDLING
REVIEWING THE ADP

Re-evaluate your key account development plan (ADP) because:

YOUR KEY ACCOUNT'S ...

- Circumstances
  - End customer wants
    - Market conditions
      - ... CAN ALL CHANGE.

Frequent reviews help you both

KEY ACCOUNT HANDLING
INTERNAL COMMUNICATION

Key account management is about:

Team meetings to involve everyone
Enthusing your colleagues
Acting as the team leader
Market research sharing
   (helps understanding)

Teamwork - you need the support of your colleagues

KEY ACCOUNT HANDLING

ACCOUNT MEETINGS (1)

Account meetings make things happen. Remember:

- **Objective** - every meeting must have one, and everyone should know it
- **Agenda** - develop it with your key account
- **Time** - allocate enough for each agenda item and cover them all
- **Participants** - should all participate?
- **Irrelevant issues** - don't allow them
- **Summarise discussion points** - to clarify understanding
- **Long meetings bore people** - keep them brief and punchy
- **Minutes** - summarise key points and action items; distribute within 48 hours
- **Finally** - if one member of the key account team goes away thinking, "I didn't get anything from this" then your meeting has failed

> Effective meeting management is the key

KEY ACCOUNT HANDLING

ACCOUNT MEETINGS (2)

Meetings for what and how often?

- Account objective setting - annually
- Business updates - every three months
- ADP reviews with key account - every three to six months
- Project review - as agreed and appropriate
- Internal review - every fortnight
- Problem solving - when required
- Proposal negotiation - as appropriate

> Meetings make things happen

KEY ACCOUNT HANDLING
ACCOUNT FOLLOW-UP

Formal follow-up

After the meeting or presentation, send an email or text within 48 hours that:
1) says thank you for the time
2) summarises points discussed
3) adds new information
4) notes the next steps

Informal follow-up

After lunch or dinner, send an email or text to say "Good seeing you".

Staying in touch

If your key account has a special interest, send an industry article that provides extra information; for example: "Sarah, I thought the enclosed article on orange plantations in South America might be of interest".

> Following-up shows you are serious

KEY ACCOUNT HANDLING

HANDING OVER AN ACCOUNT (1)

If you need to hand over your account to a colleague, then:

- Tell your key account that you've enjoyed the work
- State the reasons for the change (relocation, moving departments, etc.)
- Complete all tasks - don't leave any skeletons in the cupboard
- Go over the ADP with the new account manager
- Introduce your successor
- Tell him where to concentrate to gain an early success

When you are out ... STAY OUT!

KEY ACCOUNT HANDLING

HANDING OVER AN ACCOUNT (2)

So, your project or contract with the key account is about to end; don't delay:

- Hold a round-up meeting - ensure expectations have been met
- Ask the customer if he or she has been happy with the results; and ascertain if you are going to be asked to work for this company again and, if so, when
- Devise an appropriate contact plan, including:
  - informal meetings (think solution selling)
  - information snippets, copies of relevant press releases
  - update phone calls
  - invitations to company events
- Keep up your industry profile if you can - speak at conferences

> Stay in contact and stay patient.
> Always keep selling into other potential key accounts.
> GOOD LUCK!

About the Authors

Roger E. Jones

Roger is consulting partner for CEOs and top teams that are committed to achieving and sustaining their full potential. A best-selling author, he has conducted business in over 40 countries. His clients include senior executives in world leading companies.

He is an engaging and insightful keynote conference speaker and his work has been featured by the *BBC, Financial Times, The Sunday Times* and *Forbes*. In addition to the *Key Account Manager's Pocketbook* that he first wrote in the late 90s, he has also published *What Can Chief Executives Learn From Stand-Up Comedians* and *The Storytelling Pocketbook*.

To discover more about how Roger can assist your senior leaders and top teams, please visit www.RogerEdwardJones.com or contact him on telephone 44 (0)20 8878 3429 or email roger@RogerEdwardJones.com

Richard J. Ilsley

For the last 20 years Richard has worked at senior levels in major corporations on a range of strategic sales and marketing projects throughout the world. He has written many published texts including the book *Best Practice – A Manager's Guide (Management Books 2000)*, is an expert commentator for the national press, trade media, has spoken at conferences around the world and appeared on TV and radio.

Richard is a founder partner of Meridian, the Managing Partner of The Sales & Marketing Consulting Group and the founder of the key account esource site www.KeyAccountManagement.org.

To find out more about Richard's strategy work in sales and marketing visit www.smcg.net You can contact Richard directly at richard.ilsley@smcg.net or +44 (0) 7866 471382

Pocketbooks – *available in both paperback and digital formats*

- 360 Degree Feedback*
- Absence Management
- Appraisals
- Assertiveness
- Balance Sheet
- Body Language
- Business Planning
- Career Transition
- Coaching
- Cognitive Behavioural Coaching
- Communicator's
- Competencies
- Creative Manager's
- C.R.M.
- Cross-cultural Business
- Customer Service
- Decision-making
- Delegation
- Developing People
- Discipline & Grievance
- Diversity*
- Emotional Intelligence
- Employment Law
- Empowerment*
- Energy and Well-being
- Facilitator's
- Feedback
- Flexible Working*
- Handling Complaints
- Handling Resistance
- Icebreakers
- Impact & Presence
- Improving Efficiency
- Improving Profitability
- Induction
- Influencing
- Interviewer's
- I.T. Trainer's
- Key Account Manager's
- Leadership
- Learner's
- Management Models
- Manager's
- Managing Assessment Centres
- Managing Budgets
- Managing Cashflow
- Managing Change
- Managing Customer Service
- Managing Difficult Participants
- Managing Recruitment
- Managing Upwards
- Managing Your Appraisal
- Marketing
- Meetings
- Memory
- Mentoring
- Motivation
- Negotiator's
- Networking
- NLP
- Nurturing Innovation
- Openers & Closers
- People Manager's
- Performance Management
- Personal Success
- Positive Mental Attitude
- Presentations
- Problem Behaviour
- Problem Solving
- Project Management
- Psychometric Testing
- Resolving Conflict
- Reward
- Sales Excellence
- Salesperson's
- Self-managed Development
- Starting In Management
- Storytelling
- Strategy
- Stress
- Succeeding at Interviews
- Sustainability
- Tackling Difficult Conversations
- Talent Management
- Teambuilding Activities
- Teamworking
- Telephone Skills
- Telesales
- Thinker's
- Time Management
- Trainer's
- Training Evaluation
- Training Needs Analysis
- Transfer of Learning
- Virtual Teams
- Vocal Skills
- Working Relationships
- Workplace Politics
- Writing Skills

* only available as an e-book

Pocketfiles

Trainer's Blue Pocketfile of Ready-to-use Activities

Trainer's Green Pocketfile of Ready-to-use Activities

Trainer's Red Pocketfile of Ready-to-use Activities

To order please visit us at **www.pocketbook.co.uk**